ons— one seventeen, and ni

nd seven, years of age— They, w

their mother, constitute my whole f

y—

As to the whiskers, having never w

ny, do you not think people wou

ee it a piece of silly affecti

I were to begin it now?

Your very sincere well wis

A. Lincoln

Your very agreeable letter of the 15th is received—

I regret the necessity of saying I have no daughters— I have three sons— one seventeen, one nine, and one seven, years of age— They, with their mother, constitute my whole family—

As to the whiskers, having never worn any, do you not think people would call it a piece of silly affection

Mr Lincoln's Whiskers

Written and Illustrated by Karen Winnick

McGraw Hill SRA

Columbus, OH

MR. LINCOLN'S WHISKERS by Karen Winnick (Caroline House, an imprint of Boyds Mills Press, 1996). Reprinted with the permission of Boyds Mills Press, Inc.

For my family, Gary, Adam, Alex, Matt, and my mom.
And for my friends, Sue Alexander, Ann Paul, and Erica Silverman.
—K.W.

SRAonline.com

Mc Graw Hill SRA

Printed in the U.S.A.

Send all inquiries to:
SRA/McGraw-Hill
4400 Easton Commons
Columbus, OH 43219-6188

ISBN: 978-0-07-612521-0
MHID: 0-07-612521-1

12 13 14 15 MER 25 24 23

Grace flew down the porch steps. "Papa, how was the fair?" she asked. "Did you meet Mr. Lincoln?"

"No, Grace," Papa said. "Abraham Lincoln didn't come here to New York. He's remaining in Springfield, Illinois, during the election."

Grace's brothers and sisters greeted Papa. "Just in time for supper," Mama said.

Papa had presents for everyone. "Levant, Helen, Alice, these are for you. George, Stephen, Frank, and here's one for baby Una. And this, Grace, is for you."

"A poster of Mr. Lincoln! Oh Papa, thank you!" She held it up. Mr. Lincoln's face stared back at her.

"He looks kind," Grace thought. "Though his face seems sad."

Her brother Levant snickered. "He looks like a railsplitter, not a president."

"That's your opinion!" Grace said. "Mr. Lincoln's got a good heart. I can see it in his face. He doesn't like slavery, does he, Papa?"

"That's right," Papa said.

George, Grace's oldest brother, spoke up. "But if Lincoln's elected, our country will be split in two."

Her brother Stephen shook his head. "How's it fair for one man to own another?"

"It isn't," Grace said. "People are mean to slaves. I know about it from a book. If I could, I'd vote for Mr. Lincoln."

"It's a good thing girls can't vote," said Levant.

Grace pushed back her chair and ran out.

Alone in her room, Grace studied the poster of Mr. Lincoln. "If I could vote, I'd vote for you," she whispered.

Bright light from the moon cast deep shadows all about. A shadow fell across the poster. It made Mr. Lincoln look like he wore whiskers.

Grace stared. With his chin and the hollows of his cheeks covered, his face seemed less sad.

"What if . . .?" Grace thought.

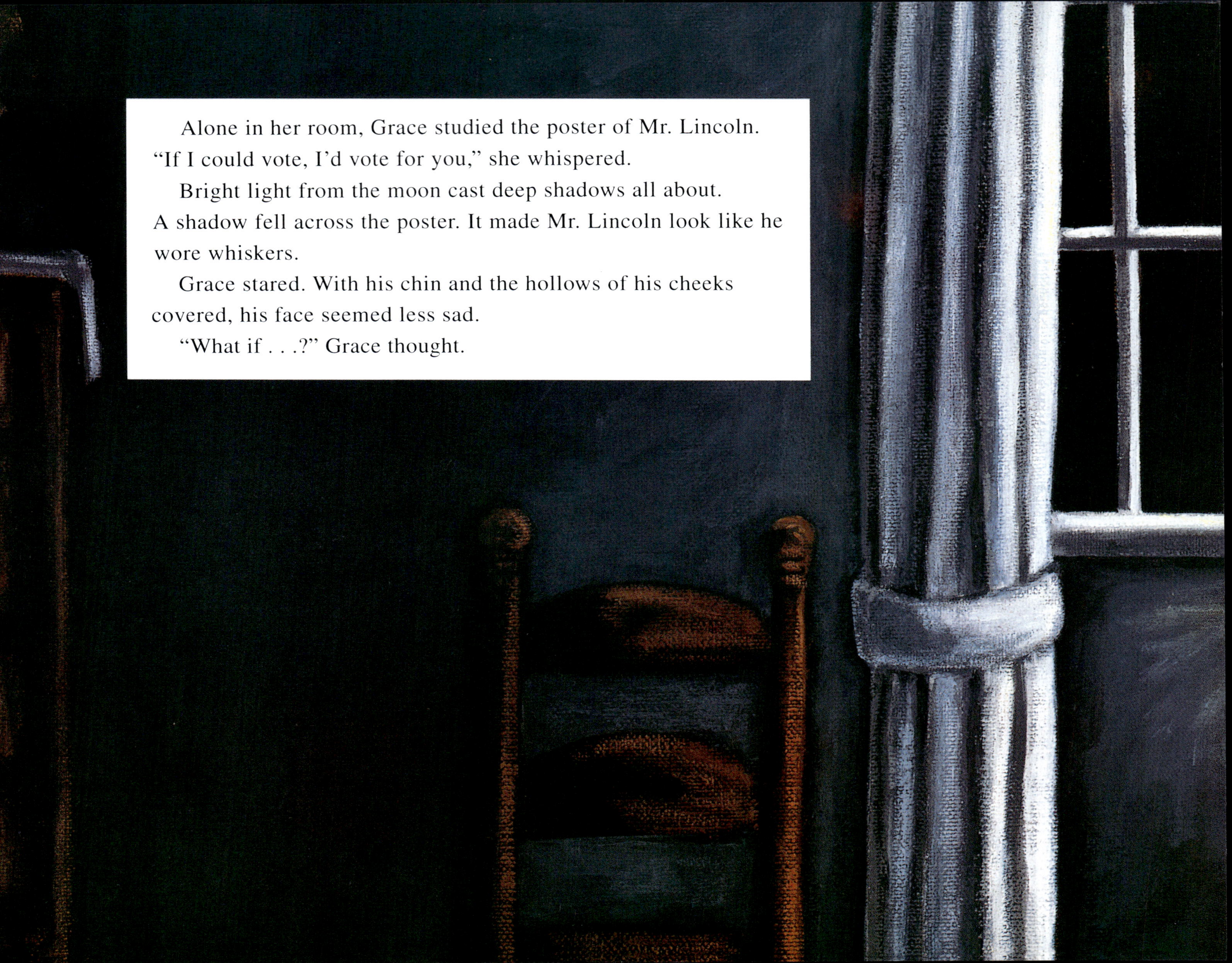

She hurried over to her desk. She took a sheet of paper and dipped her feather-quill pen into a pot of ink.

By the light of the moon she wrote . . .

Hon. A.B. Lincoln

Dear Sir:

My father has just come from the fair and brought home your picture . . . I am a little girl only eleven years old, but want you should be President of the United States very much so I hope you won't think me very bold to write to such a great man as you are. Have you any little girls about as large as I am if so give them my love and tell her to write to me if you cannot answer this letter: I have got 4 brothers and part of them will vote for you anyway and if you will let your whiskers grow I will try and get the rest of them to vote for you. You would look a great deal better for your face is so thin. All the ladies like whiskers and they would tease their husbands to vote for you and then you would be President. My father is going to vote for you and if I was a man I would vote for you too but I will try and get every one to vote for you that I can . . . I must not write any more. Answer this letter right off. Good-bye

Grace Bedell

Grace addressed the envelope. "Springfield, Illinois, that's where Papa said he'd be." She put the letter in the envelope and tucked it under her pillow. They she climbed into bed.

In the morning, Grace hurried to mail the letter before going to school. She kept it hidden under her cape. If Levant knew she had written to Mr. Lincoln, he would laugh.

Just before the post office on Main Street, Grace stopped. Should she send the letter? Wouldn't it seem foolish, a small girl writing to such a great man?

No, she decided, she had made a good suggestion.

She went inside the post office. "May I have a stamp, Mr. Mann?" She handed the postmaster a penny and her letter.

"To Mr. Abraham Lincoln?" Mr. Mann exclaimed. "Why, Grace Bedell, did you write this yourself?"

She blushed and nodded.

"Well," he said, "I wouldn't expect an answer. Mr. Lincoln's a busy man.

Grace's shoulders drooped. She turned and walked slowly out of the post office.

A few days later she returned.

"Is there anything for me?"

"No," said Mr. Mann. "I told you Mr. Lincoln was very busy."

But the next day she trudged back and the day after that.

On the seventh day after she sent her letter, Grace headed toward the post office. Light snowflakes were falling.

A crowd stood in front of the building. They talked in excited whispers. A man pointed, "Here's Grace," he said.

Mr. Mann rushed outside waving an envelope. "Your letter came! From Mr. Lincoln! Imagine, at our post office in Westfield!"

Grace took the letter. Her heart beat fast as she opened the envelope.

"What did Mr. Lincoln write?" a boy asked.

But Grace was already hurrying home, reading her letter.

She burst into the parlor. "Mr. Lincoln answered my letter!"

Mama looked up. "You wrote to Mr. Lincoln?"

Her brothers and sisters gathered around. "What did you say?" "Where did you send it?"

Papa put down his pipe."Read us what he wrote, Grace."

She held up the letter. Spots from the melted snow dotted the paper. Grace read aloud:

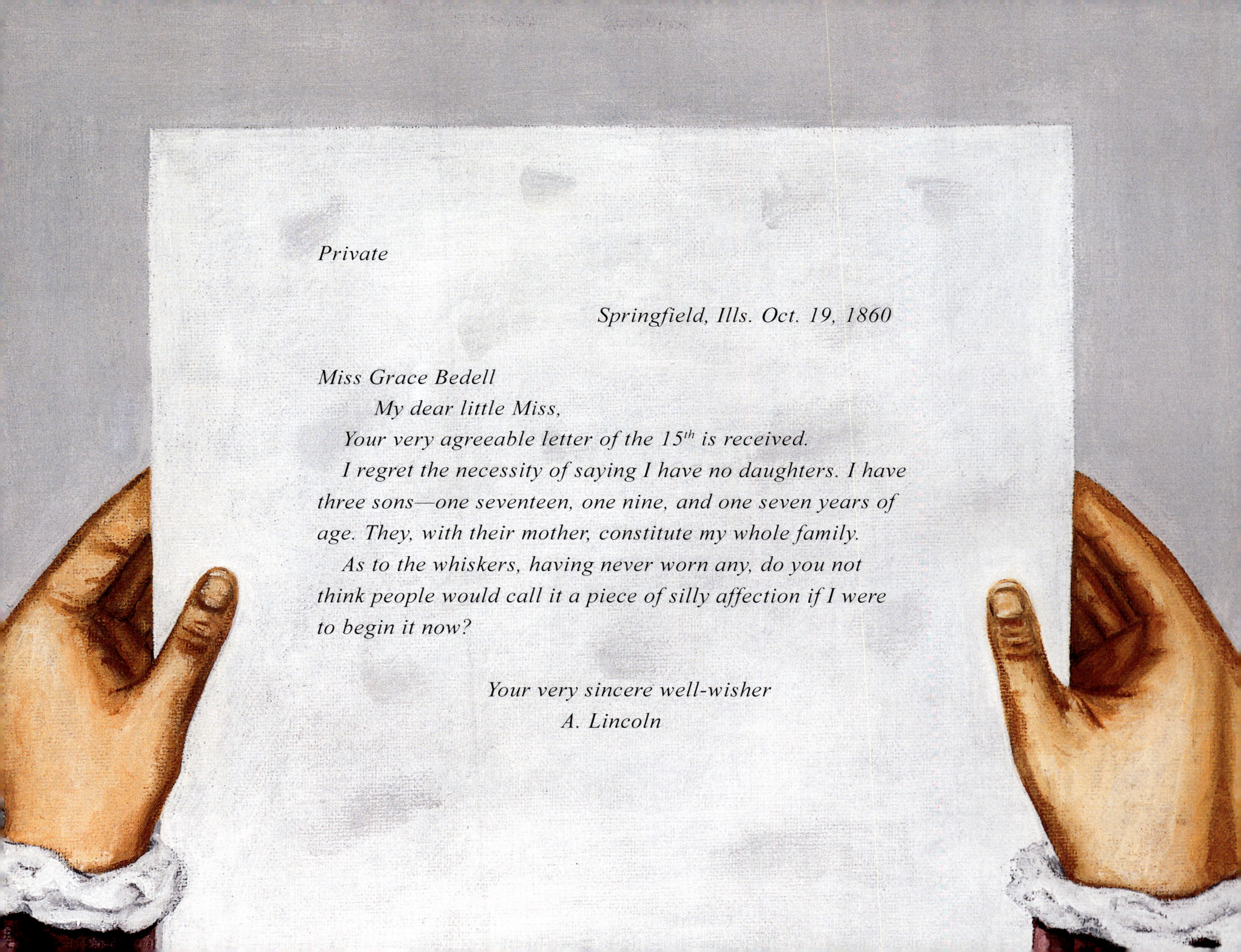

Private

Springfield, Ills. Oct. 19, 1860

Miss Grace Bedell

My dear little Miss,

Your very agreeable letter of the 15th is received.

I regret the necessity of saying I have no daughters. I have three sons—one seventeen, one nine, and one seven years of age. They, with their mother, constitute my whole family.

As to the whiskers, having never worn any, do you not think people would call it a piece of silly affection if I were to begin it now?

Your very sincere well-wisher

A. Lincoln

Levant made a face. "You wrote him about growing whiskers?"
"I can't believe it!" Mama said. "Mr. Lincoln wrote to our Grace."
"You should be very proud," Papa said.

On Election Day, Grace watched Papa and her brothers go off to cast their votes. "Oh, I hope Mr. Lincoln wins," she thought.

Late the following day, people were shouting in the streets. "The telegraph says Mr. Lincoln is winning! He's going to be our next president!" Grace and Papa hugged each other.

A month later Papa sat in the parlor reading his newspaper. He looked up. “Listen to this,” he said. “Abraham Lincoln will be traveling from Springfield to Washington, D.C., to be sworn into office. His train will stop for wood and water right here in Westfield.”

Grace jumped out of her chair. “Can we go to the station?” she asked. “I want to see Mr. Lincoln.”

“After writing him such a foolish letter?” asked Levant.

The wind whistled across the tracks. Grace pushed her hands into her muff. She blew out a stream of air.

There was a faint chug-a-chug.

Grace squeezed forward. Mama touched her shoulder and pulled her back. "Stay close."

"But I want to see Mr. Lincoln," Grace said.

The chug-a-chug got louder and louder. A bell rang. Gray clouds rose from the engine's smoke stack. People shouted and waved flags. The long, dark train drew into the station.

Grace stood on her toes but she couldn't see above the stovepipe hats and feathered bonnets. Where was Mr. Lincoln? Was he speaking? She couldn't hear with all the clapping and cheering.

Suddenly, people began to turn around. "Where is she?" "Where is she?" Grace heard them murmur.

"Grace! Grace!" Mr. Mann pushed through the crowd. "Mr. Lincoln wants to see you." Mr. Mann took her arm.

Everyone hurried to move out of her way. Grace could hear their whispering as she went past. Mr. Mann led her to the front of the platform.

Abraham Lincoln stood before her.

"Hello, Grace," he said. "How do you like the improvement you advised me to make?"

Mr. Lincoln bent down and gave her a kiss. His whiskers tickled her cheek.

In October, 1860, Grace Bedell of Westfield, New York wrote to Abraham Lincoln advising him to grow a beard. These are reproductions of the letters they exchanged.

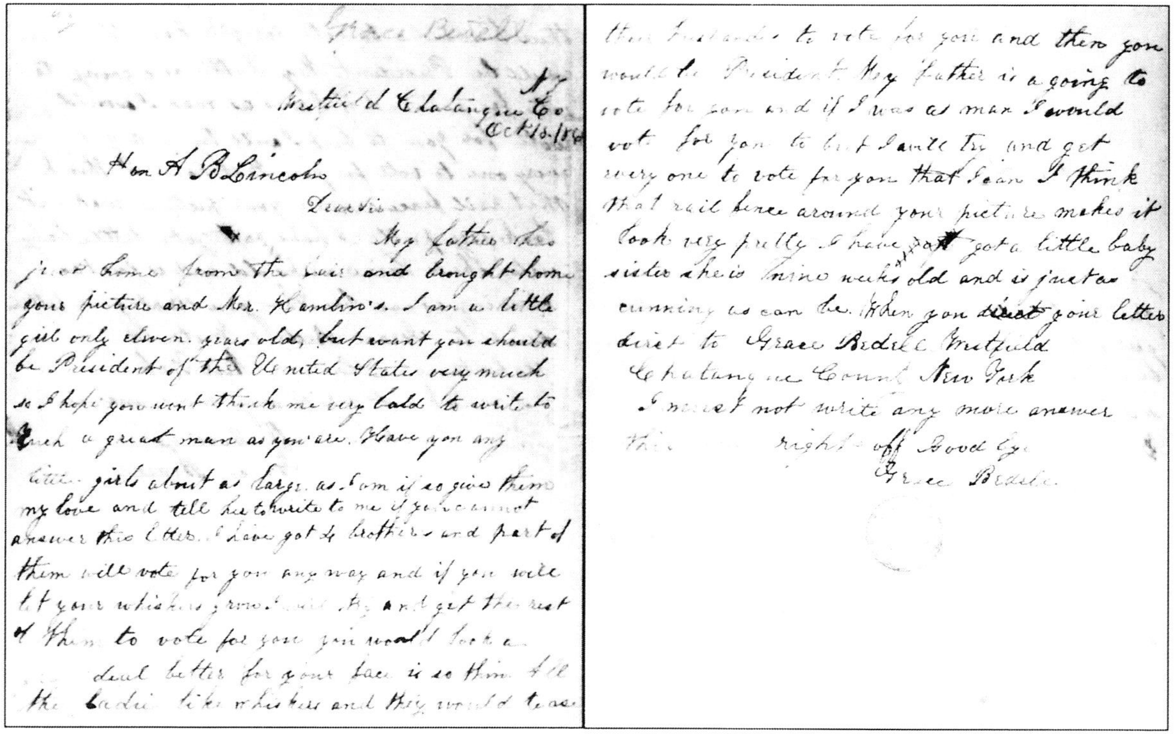

Grace Bedell

N Y
Westfield Chatauque Co
Oct 15. 1860

Hon A B Lincoln

Dear Sir

My father has just home from the fair and brought home your picture and Mr. Hamlin's. I am a little girl only eleven years old, but want you should be President of the United States very much so I hope you wont think me very bold to write to such a great man as you are. Have you any little girls about as large as I am if so give them my love and tell her to write to me if you cannot answer this letter. I have got 4 brothers and part of them will vote for you any way and if you will let your whiskers grow I will try and get the rest of them to vote for you you would look a great deal better for your face is so thin. All the ladies like whiskers and they would tease their husbands to vote for you and then you would be President. My father is a going to vote for you and if I was a man I would vote for you to but I will try and get every one to vote for you that I can I think that rail fence around your picture makes it look very pretty I have got a little baby sister she is nine weeks old and is just as cunning as can be. When you direct your letter direct to Grace Bedell Westfield Chatauque County New York

I must not write any more answer this letter right off Good bye

Grace Bedell

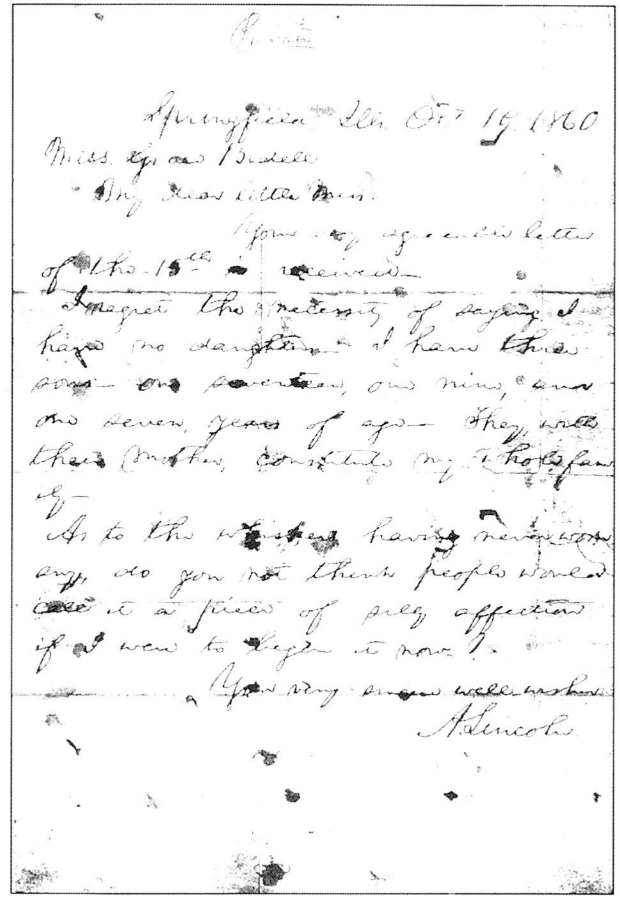

Private

Springfield, Ills. Oct 19. 1860

Miss. Grace Bedell

My dear little Miss.

Your very agreeable letter of the 15th. is received.

I regret the necessity of saying I have no daughters. I have three sons—one seventeen, one nine, and one seven, years of age. They, with their mother, constitute my whole family.

As to the whiskers, having never worn any, do you not think people would call it a piece of silly affection if I were to begin it now?

Your very sincere well-wisher

A. Lincoln.

...s — one seventeen, one nine, an...

...o seven, years of age — They, wi...

...er mother, constitute my whole f...

—

As to the whiskers, having never w...

...y do you not think people wou...

...e it a piece of silly affectation...

...I were to begin it now?

Your very sincere well-wish...

A. Lincoln

Your very agreeable letter
of the 15th. is received —
I regret the necessity of saying I
have no daughters — I have three
sons — one seventeen, one nine, and
one seven, years of age — They, with
their mother, constitute my whole fam-
ily —
As to the whiskers, having never wo[rn]
any, do you not think people would
call it a piece of silly affectation